# WILD ANIMALS

# TASMANIAN DEVILS

BY DALTON RAINS

# WWW.APEXEDITIONS.COM

Copyright © 2026 by Apex Editions, Mendota Heights, MN 55120. All rights reserved. No part of this book may be reproduced or utilized in any form or by any means without written permission from the publisher.

Apex is distributed by North Star Editions:
sales@northstareditions.com | 888-417-0195

Produced for Apex by Red Line Editorial.

Photographs ©: Shutterstock Images, cover, 1, 4–5, 7, 8–9, 10–11, 12, 14–15, 18, 19, 20–21, 24–25, 29; iStockphoto, 6, 16–17, 27; Geoffrey Lea/Auscape International Pty Ltd/Alamy, 22–23

**Library of Congress Control Number: 2025930912**

**ISBN**
979-8-89250-552-9 (hardcover)
979-8-89250-588-8 (paperback)
979-8-89250-656-4 (ebook pdf)
979-8-89250-624-3 (hosted ebook)

Printed in the United States of America
Mankato, MN
082025

## NOTE TO PARENTS AND EDUCATORS

**Apex books are designed to build literacy skills in striving readers. Exciting, high-interest content attracts and holds readers' attention. The text is carefully leveled to allow students to achieve success quickly. Additional features, such as bolded glossary words for difficult terms, help build comprehension.**

# TABLE OF CONTENTS

**CHAPTER 1**
FOOD FIGHT 4

**CHAPTER 2**
TEARING TEETH 10

**CHAPTER 3**
GROSS MEALS 16

**CHAPTER 4**
LIFE CYCLE 22

COMPREHENSION QUESTIONS • 28
GLOSSARY • 30
TO LEARN MORE • 31
ABOUT THE AUTHOR • 31
INDEX • 32

CHAPTER 1

# FOOD FIGHT

It's a quiet night in the forest. A Tasmanian devil searches for a meal. Soon, it finds a dead animal. The devil's sharp teeth tear into the body.

A Tasmanian devil's bite can crush bone.

Another Tasmanian devil arrives. It bares its teeth. Then it pushes the first devil out of the way. Both animals want the meatiest parts.

**Tasmanian devils let out loud screeches and growls when fighting for food.**

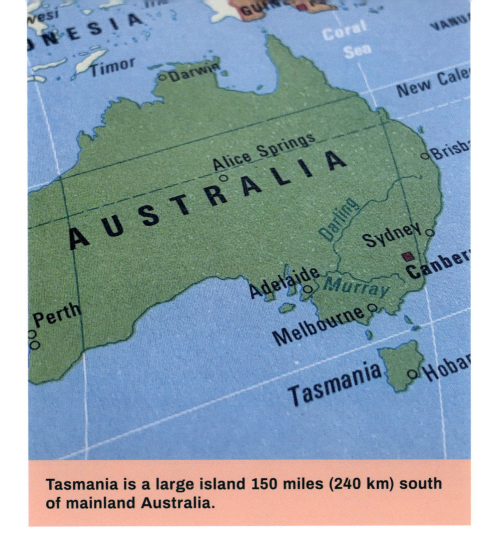

Tasmania is a large island 150 miles (240 km) south of mainland Australia.

## SCARY SOUNDS

When Europeans first came to Tasmania, they heard animal sounds in the forests. The Europeans thought the noises sounded like devils. That's how the Tasmanian devil got its name.

More devils arrive. Their calls spread through the forest. Each devil wants its fill. Soon, they devour the entire animal.

FAST FACT

Tasmanian devils will eat all parts of an animal, including hair, **organs**, and bones.

A Tasmanian devil can eat nearly half of its body weight in a day.

CHAPTER 2

# Tearing Teeth

**T**asmanian devils are **marsupials**. The animals have brown or black fur. Their chests have white stripes or patches. Devils also have long tails.

Adult Tasmanian devils are about 30 inches (76 cm) long. They weigh up to 26 pounds (12 kg).

Devils have big heads and strong **jaws**. They have some of the most powerful bites of any animal. Tasmanian devils have even been known to bite through metal.

FAST FACT
Over time, the sharp edges of a Tasmanian devil's teeth wear down.

◀ **A Tasmanian devil uses large front teeth to stab. Thick back teeth crush bone and tear skin.**

Long whiskers help devils sense things in the dark. The animals also have great hearing and smell. Devils use these senses to find food and avoid **predators**.

## FAST MOVERS

Tasmanian devils can reach speeds of 15 miles per hour (24 km/h). Their claws help them move over rough ground. Devils are also good at swimming and climbing.

When in danger, Tasmanian devils tend to run away rather than fight.

CHAPTER 3

# GROSS MEALS

Tasmanian devils are solitary. They spend most of their time alone. The animals sleep through the day. They come out to feed at night.

Tasmanian devils sleep in holes, caves, or hollow logs.

A Tasmanian devil stores fat in its tail. That helps it survive when there is not much food.

Devils are **carnivores**. They usually find dead animals to eat. But sometimes they hunt small **prey**. For example, devils may hunt frogs, birds, fish, or insects.

**FAST FACT**
A tired devil may sleep inside a rotting body. When the devil wakes up, it gets back to eating.

Tasmanian devils travel up to 10 miles (16 km) each night looking for food.

Farmers killed many devils in the late 1800s. They didn't want devils to kill their farm animals. Today, laws protect devils. But the animals remain **endangered**.

## DEADLY DISEASE

Many Tasmanian devils get a deadly disease. It spreads when they bite one another. In 1996, there were more than 150,000 devils in the wild. By 2020, fewer than 17,000 remained.

Tasmanian devils hunt small animals that eat crops. So, devils can be helpful to farmers.

CHAPTER 4

# Life Cycle

**T**asmanian devils **mate** in summer or fall. About 3 weeks after mating, a female has 20 or more tiny babies. They race to a pouch on their mother's belly.

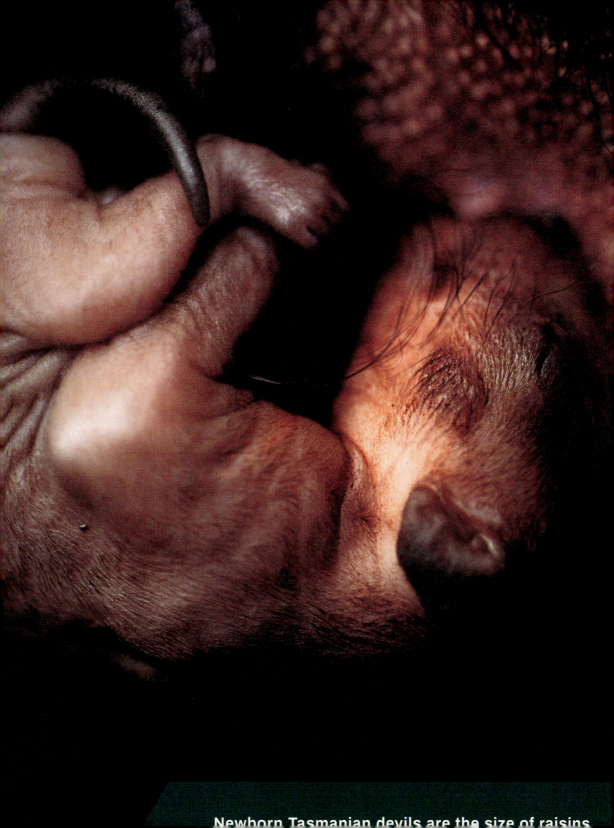

Newborn Tasmanian devils are the size of raisins

The babies grow by drinking milk from their mother's body. However, she has only four nipples. So, only the quickest of the babies survive. After about four months, they leave the pouch.

**FAST FACT**

Young devils may stay in a **den** while their mother hunts.

A Tasmanian devil weighs about 7 ounces (200 g) when it leaves the pouch.

After eight months, the devils leave their mother. But many of the young animals have trouble getting enough food. Only 4 in 10 survive more than a few months.

## DEVIL DANGER

When hungry, adult Tasmanian devils sometimes eat younger devils. But the young animals are quicker than adults. They can also climb trees. That helps them escape.

Tasmanian devils can live for five years or more in the wild.

# COMPREHENSION QUESTIONS

*Write your answers on a separate piece of paper.*

1. Write a few sentences explaining the main ideas of Chapter 3.

2. What feature of Tasmanian devils do you find most interesting? Why?

3. At what age does a Tasmanian devil leave its mother's pouch?

    **A.** three weeks old
    **B.** four months old
    **C.** eight months old

4. By how much did the Tasmanian devil population shrink from 1996 to 2020?

    **A.** less than 100,000
    **B.** about 130,000
    **C.** more than 150,000

**5.** What does **devour** mean in this book?

*Each devil wants its fill. Soon, they devour the entire animal.*

- **A.** to eat plants
- **B.** to eat alone
- **C.** to eat quickly

**6.** What does **solitary** mean in this book?

*Tasmanian devils are solitary. They spend most of their time alone.*

- **A.** not part of a group
- **B.** always with other animals
- **C.** not able to move at night

*Answer key on page 32.*

29

# GLOSSARY

**carnivores**
Animals that eat meat.

**den**
The home of a wild animal.

**endangered**
In danger of dying out forever.

**jaws**
The two bones that form an animal's mouth.

**marsupials**
Types of mammals that often have pouches for their young.

**mate**
To form a pair and come together to have babies.

**organs**
Parts of the body that do certain jobs. Organs include the heart, lungs, and kidneys.

**predators**
Animals that hunt and eat other animals.

**prey**
Animals that are hunted and eaten by other animals.

# TO LEARN MORE

## BOOKS

Grack, Rachel. *Tasmanian Devils*. Bellwether Media, 2023.

Klepinger, Teresa. *Wolverine vs. Tasmanian Devil*. Kaleidoscope, 2023.

Markle, Sandra. *Tasmanian Devils: Nature's Cleanup Crew*. Lerner Publications, 2024.

## ONLINE RESOURCES

Visit **www.apexeditions.com** to find links and resources related to this title.

## ABOUT THE AUTHOR

Dalton Rains is an author and editor from Saint Paul, Minnesota.

# INDEX

**B**
babies, 22, 24
biting, 13, 20

**C**
carnivores, 18
climbing, 14, 26

**D**
den, 24
disease, 20

**E**
endangered, 20
Europeans, 7

**F**
fur, 10

**J**
jaws, 13

**M**
marsupials, 10
mating, 22
mother, 22, 24, 26

**P**
pouch, 22, 24

**T**
tails, 10
Tasmania, 7
teeth, 4, 6, 13

**W**
whiskers, 14

**ANSWER KEY:**
1. Answers will vary; 2. Answers will vary; 3. B; 4. B; 5. C; 6. A